MATH ADVENTURES

Firefighters to the Rescue

by Wendy Clemson and David Clemson

Math and curriculum consultant: Debra Voege, M.A., science and math curriculum resource teacher

GARETH**STEVENS**
GS

Please visit our web site at: **www.garethstevens.com**
For a free color catalog describing Gareth Stevens Publishing's list of high-quality books
and multimedia programs, call 1-800-542-2595 (USA) or 1-800-387-3178 (Canada).
Gareth Stevens Publishing's fax: (414) 332-3567

Library of Congress Cataloging-in-Publication Data

Clemson, Wendy.
    Firefighters to the rescue / Wendy Clemson and David Clemson. — North American ed.
        p. cm. — (Math adventures)
    ISBN-13: 978-0-8368-7839-4 (lib. bdg.)
    ISBN-13: 978-0-8368-8138-7 (softcover)
    1. Mathematics—Problems, exercises, etc.—Juvenile literature.
    2. Fire fighters—Juvenile literature. I. Clemson, David. II. Title.
    QA43.C656   2006
    510—dc22
                                                2006052247

This North American edition first published in 2007 by
Gareth Stevens Publishing
A Member of the WRC Media Family of Companies
330 West Olive Street, Suite 100
Milwaukee, WI 53212 USA

This U.S. edition copyright © 2007 by Gareth Stevens, Inc. Original edition copyright © 2007 by
ticktock Entertainment Ltd. First published in Great Britain in 2006 by ticktock Media Ltd., Unit 2,
Orchard Business Centre, North Farm Road, Tunbridge Wells, Kent, TN2 3XF.

ticktock project editor: Rebecca Clunes
ticktock project designer: Sara Greasley
Gareth Stevens editor: Tea Benduhn
Gareth Stevens art direction: Tammy West
Gareth Stevens graphic designer: Kami Strunsee
Gareth Stevens production: Jessica Yanke and Robert Kraus

Picture credits
t=top, b=bottom, c=center, l=left, r=right
Peter Casolino/Alamy 10b; Comstock Images/Alamy 1, 5; FEMA/Andrea Booher 14-15; FEMA/Justin Domeroski 16;
FEMA/Bob McMillan 17; Jiang Jin/SuperStock 25; Shutterstock 2, 4 (all), 6-7, 8, 9, 10t, 12-13, 18-19, 20, 21, 22t,
22b, 23, 24, 26t, 26b, 27, 28, 29, 30, 31t, 31b, 32.

Printed in Canada

1 2 3 4 5 6 7 8 9 10 10 09 08 07 06

CONTENTS

MEASUREMENT CONVERSIONS

1 inch = 2.5 centimeters

1 foot = 0.3 meter

1 mile = 1.6 kilometers

1 square mile = 2.6 square kilometers

1 pound = 0.5 kilogram

1 gallon = 3.8 liters

WELCOME TO THE FIRE STATION

You have a dangerous but rewarding job. You are a firefighter at a busy fire station. You help put out fires and rescue people in trouble. Your skills and bravery save lives, and helping other people makes you feel good.

Fighting fires is an exciting and important job.

Firefighters teach people about how fires start and how to keep them from starting.

Most of the fires that firefighters put out are in homes, stores, and offices.

Firefighters also put out fires in forests and in the countryside.

Sometimes firefighters talk to children about their jobs.

Did you know that firefighters need to use math?

Inside this book, you will find math puzzles that firefighters have to solve every day. You will also have a chance to answer number questions about fires, firefighters, and fire safety.

What is inside the book?

Charts and tables will help you answer the math questions.

Find out what needs to be done in your busy day.

Fact boxes tell you more about a firefighter's duties.

Answer the questions and practice your math skills.

If you get stuck, there are some tips to help you on pages 30 and 31.

Are you ready to be a firefighter for the day?

You will need paper, a pencil, and a ruler, and don't forget to wear your firefighting uniform. Let's go!

YOUR FIRE STATION

You are a firefighter for one of your city's fire stations. You fight many kinds of fires. Some fires happen in people's homes. Others happen in the countryside. You could be called to a fire at any time.

The firefighters at your station have the following duties:
2 fire chiefs: decide how to put out a fire
2 crew leaders: organize the firefighters
12 firefighters: fight the fire and put it out

1 If the firefighters at your station work in two equal teams, how many people are in each team?

2 Your station is always busy. Last year, you put out 130 big fires and 100 small fires. How many more big fires did you put out than small fires?

3 Last year, your team put out 60 car fires and 15 house fires. What is the total number of car and house fires?

WHERE IS THE FIRE?

The graph to the right shows the number of fires last week.

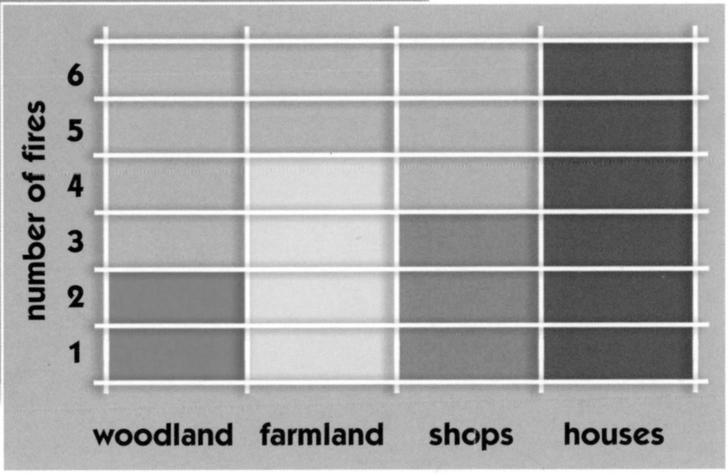

number of fires

6
5
4
3
2
1

woodland   farmland   shops   houses

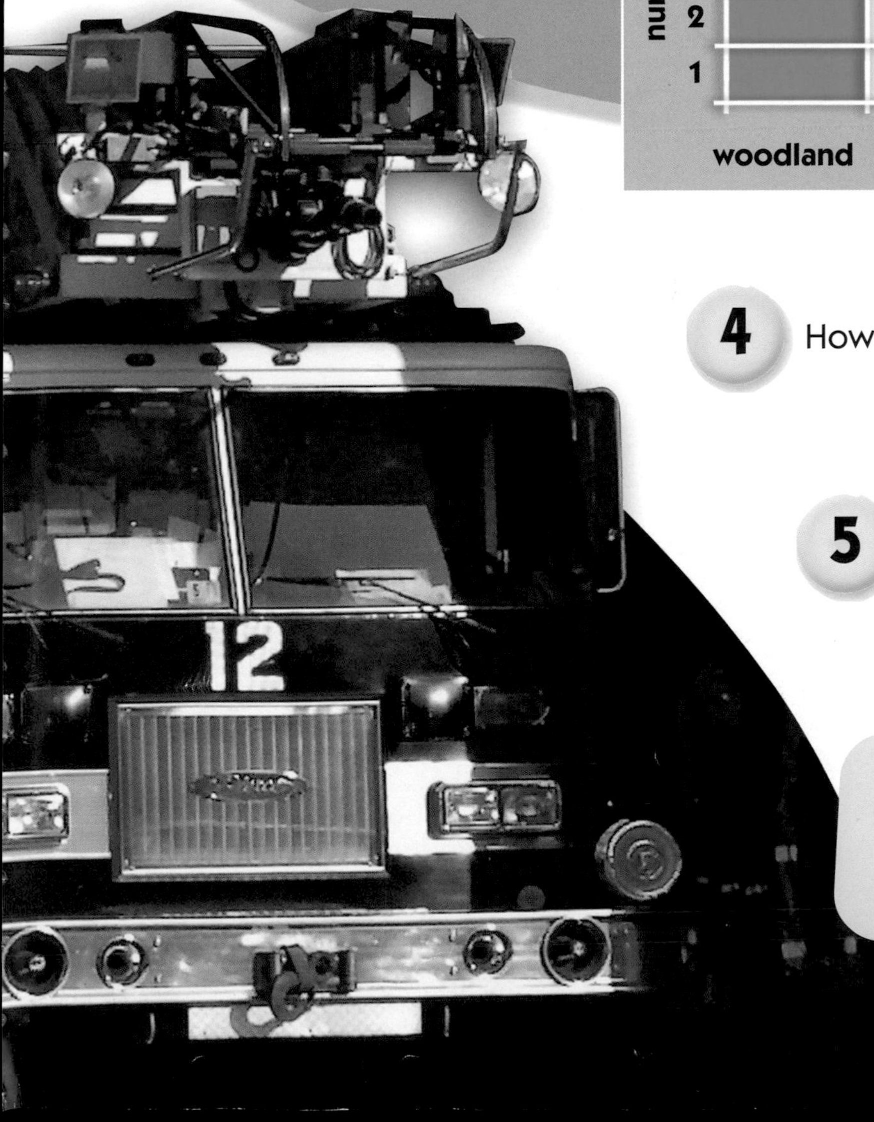

4 How many fires were on farmland?

5 How many fires were there in total?

Most fire stations have at least two fire engines.

12

STARTING YOUR SHIFT

When you arrive at work, there are always lots of things to do, even when there are no fires. You keep the fire station clean and tidy. You also make sure that everything on the fire engine works well.

Firefighters are needed day and night. They work in shifts. A shift is the time that a firefighter spends at work. A firefighter can work a day shift or a night shift.

1 This week, you will work 4 day shifts. How many days in the week are you not working a day shift?

2 The clock to the left shows the time you start work in the morning. What time do you start work?

YESTERDAY'S TIMETABLE

You were not called out to a fire yesterday. The table below shows some things you did instead.

9:00 – 10:30	checking the engine
10:30 – 11:00	taking a break
11:00 – 12:00	fire training
12:00 – 1:00	cleaning equipment
1:00 – 2:00	eating lunch

3 What were you doing at 10:00?

4 What were you doing at 11:30?

5 What were you doing at 1:15?

6 After lunch, you spent another hour cleaning equipment. Then, you showed a group of children around the fire station until the end of your shift. You finished work at 5:00 p.m. How long did the children visit the station?

NEW CLOTHES

Today, you will get a new uniform! The storage room has lots of helmets, trousers, and jackets. You choose the clothes that fit you best.

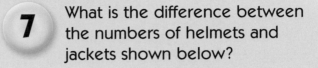

7 What is the difference between the numbers of helmets and jackets shown below?

8 What is the difference between the numbers of trousers and jackets?

14 helmets   **36 trousers**   **18 jackets**

Their uniforms protect firefighters from the heat of a fire. The uniforms are waterproof, too!

9

THE ALARM CALL

Someone has dialed 911. There is a fire somewhere in the city! The alarm bell at the fire station rings. All the firefighters jump up and rush to the fire engine. It takes just 60 seconds for you to put on your uniform and climb into the engine. You are ready to roll!

You need to get from the fire station to the fire in 10 minutes.

1 Which of the math puzzles below have the answer 10?

A
1+2+3+4

B
2+2+2+2+2+2

C
180 – 160

D
30 – 3

E
2 x 5

2 A fire in the countryside takes 20 minutes to get to. How many groups of 2 are in 20?

Specially trained operators take 911 calls. They find out the details of the emergency and then let the fire station know.

3 When the alarm bell sounds, it takes the firefighters 1 minute to get to the fire engine. After getting to the engine, the driver takes 2 minutes to leave the station. It then takes 3 minutes to reach the main road. How long has it been since the alarm bell first rang?

WHERE IS THE FIRE?

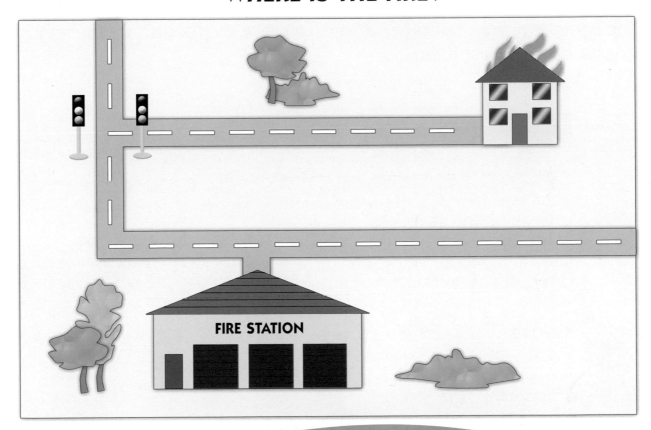

4 Look at the map above. You need to give the driver directions to get from the fire station to the fire. Would you choose A, B, or C from the directions below?

A   Turn left out of the station, then turn left again.
    Go past the traffic lights, then turn right.

B   Turn right out of the station, then turn left.
    Go past the traffic lights, then turn left.

C   Turn left out of the station, then turn right.
    At the traffic lights, turn right.

GETTING TO THE FIRE

The fire engine leaves the station. You are on your way! The engine races through traffic. Its lights flash, and its siren makes a loud noise. The lights and siren tell other drivers to move to the side so your fire engine can get past them.

1 Look at the line of vehicles above. How many vehicles need to move out of the way to let your fire engine through?

2 Your fire engine can go about 1 mile in 3 minutes. How far can it go in 6 minutes?

3 The lights on your fire engine flash 60 times in 1 minute. How many times do the lights flash in 1½ minutes?

The diagram to the right has 16 squares.

1	2		4
5		7	8
9	10	11	
	14	15	16

4 What is on square 13 of the diagram?

5 What is on square 3 of the diagram?

6 Which square is the house on?

7 What is to the left of square 7 on the diagram?

KEY

 = tree

 = campfire

 = fire engine

 = house

Firefighters are specially trained to drive safely at high speeds.

FOREST FIRE

There is a fire in the woods. The risk of fires in forests is very high in hot, dry weather. The dry wood and leaves mean there is lots of fuel for the fire. A strong wind can make a forest fire spread very quickly.

Standing in front of a fire is very dangerous if the wind is pushing the fire toward you. Firefighters have to find out which direction the wind is blowing.

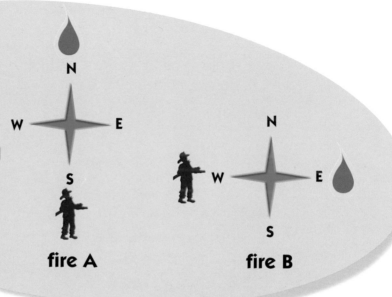

fire A

fire B

1 Look at fire A above. The wind is blowing from north to south. Is the firefighter safe?

2 At fire B above, the wind is blowing from west to east. Is the firefighter safe?

A big wildfire can burn 1½ square miles in 1 hour.

A FIRE PICTOGRAM

Firefighters look for clues to figure out how a fire started. The pictogram to the left shows how forest fires started last year.

how fires started	number of fires
lightning strike	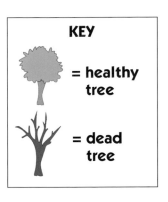
campfire	
deliberately started	

= 2 fires

3 How did most of the fires start?

4 How many fires were there in total?

5 Some trees die after a forest fire, but others recover and have new leaves in spring. How many of the trees below are dead?

KEY

= healthy tree

= dead tree

ON THE ENGINE

Your fire engine has all of the equipment you need to fight a forest fire. It carries long hoses, different kinds of ladders, and 500 gallons of water. The fire engine also has powerful lights to help the firefighters see better when they work in the dark.

The fire engine has 2 ladders. One is 44 feet long, and the other is 34 feet long.

1 How much higher than the shorter ladder can the longer ladder reach?

On the ladder to the right, you can see the first 8 rungs.

2 You are standing on rung 4 and move down 2 rungs. Which rung are you standing on now?

3 You are on rung 3 and climb up 5 rungs. Which rung are you on now?

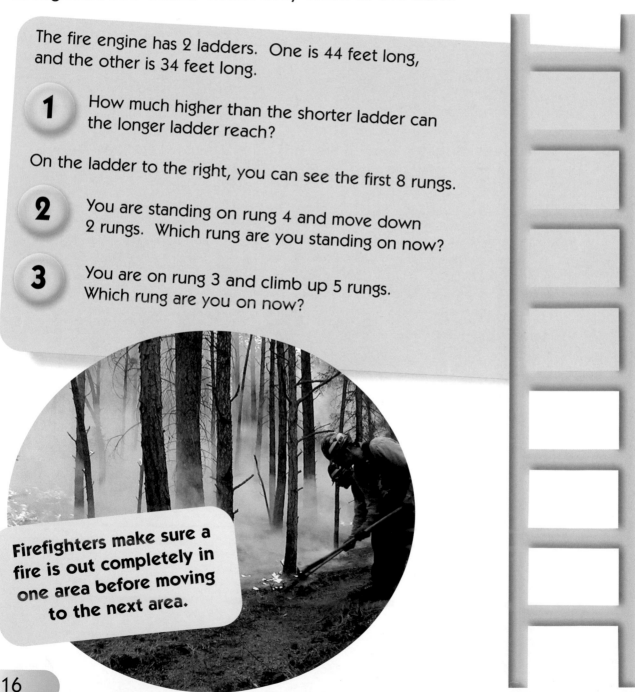

Firefighters make sure a fire is out completely in one area before moving to the next area.

Some fire engines carry more than 1/2 mile of hose.

4 The engine can pump 5 gallons of water in 1 second. How much water does the engine pump in 3 seconds?

THE WATER TRUCK

The fire station has a special truck that only carries water. The water truck can carry more than 1,000 gallons of water! That is much more water than the fire engine can carry alone.

5 Fire engines have 2 hoses. Water trucks have 5 hoses. How many hoses are on 2 fire engines and 1 water truck?

The forest fire is out, but the fire station calls you again. There is a house fire in town. They need you to go there right away!

RESCUE

You arrive at the house fire. Before you start fighting the fire, you make sure everyone is safe. Then you need to find out where the fire is coming from and put the fire out.

The house to the right is on fire. You talk with your chief and agree on the best way to fight the fire.

 1 Name the following shapes on the house:

A roof

B door

C top windows

D window to the left of the door

E window to the right of the door

Everyone is safely out of the house. But wait! You hear a barking sound. Rusty the dog is trapped upstairs. You quickly climb your ladder to go rescue him!

You take: 2 minutes to go up the ladder, 3 minutes to go through the house, 1 minute to pick up Rusty, and 2 minutes to carry Rusty to safety.

2 How long does it take you to rescue Rusty?

3 Rusty is heavy! After the rescue, you put him on the scale to the right to see how much he weighs. How much does Rusty weigh?

4 Most people weigh more than dogs. You once carried a woman from a burning building. She weighed the same amount as 3 Rustys! How much did the woman weigh?

A fire can grow quickly. It can double in size every minute.

Your gloves have an inside layer that protects your hands from heat.

5 The glove to the right shows the back of one of your gloves. Is it for your right hand or your left hand?

PUTTING OUT THE FIRE

There is no one in the house now so you can concentrate on putting out the flames. You use lots of water. The water is pumped through a hose. You point the hose at the bottom of the fire to put out its source. Soon, the fire is out.

Firefighters sometimes take water from nearby ponds.

1 Your red hoses are 50 feet long. Your black hoses are 100 feet long. You can attach them together to make a longer hose. If you use the fewest number of hoses, how many of each hose would make a hose that measures 150 feet long?

2 Using the fewest number of hoses, how would you make a hose that measures 300 feet long?

3 Firefighters can choose the width of the hose as well as its length. The hose to the right has the smallest width. Use a ruler to measure it. How wide is the hose?

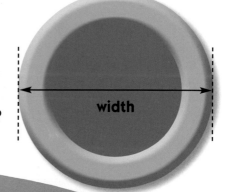

width

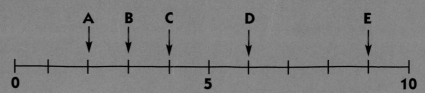

4 Wider hoses will pump more water onto a fire. One hose is 4 inches wide, and another is 5 inches wide. Look at the number line below. Which letter marks the number 4?

5 What number does the letter D mark?

```
      A    B    C         D              E
      |    |    |         |              |
      ↓    ↓    ↓         ↓              ↓
  |--+--+--+--+--+--+--+--+--+--+--|
  0              5                    10
```

Firefighters can control the amount of water flowing through the hose and the pattern of the spray.

CLEANUP TIME

The fire is out, but is it safe to go back into the house? You and your team have to make sure there is no chance of another fire starting. You also have to make sure the house is safe for people to go back inside.

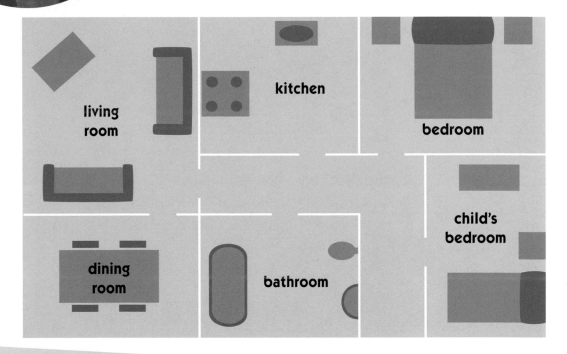

1 The picture above shows a floor plan of the house. You make sure the fire is out in every room. How many rooms do you check?

2 You check the kitchen first, then the living room, dining room, and bathroom. Are you going clockwise or counterclockwise?

3 What fraction of the rooms in this house are bedrooms?
   A ½   B ⅓   C ¼

After the fire, there are lots of burned things to throw away. You help by putting trash into the containers below.

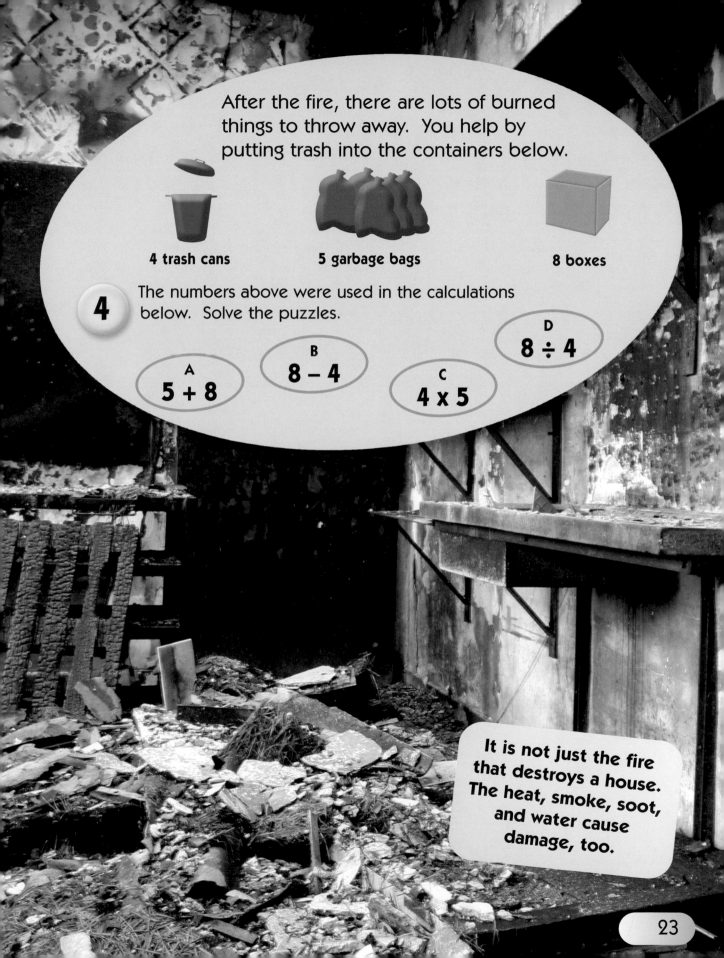

4 trash cans

5 garbage bags

8 boxes

4 The numbers above were used in the calculations below. Solve the puzzles.

A
5 + 8

B
8 − 4

C
4 x 5

D
8 ÷ 4

It is not just the fire that destroys a house. The heat, smoke, soot, and water cause damage, too.

AFTER WORK – STAYING FIT

Firefighters need to be strong and healthy. Each day, they have to bend, stretch, lift, and carry heavy objects. After work, you exercise to make sure you stay strong and healthy.

1 You need hand weights to lift. You want to buy a new set. You want a set that costs less than $35 and is not heavier than 10 pounds. From the sets in the table below, which set best suits your needs?

	cost	weight
set 1	$25	11 pounds
set 2	$40	9 pounds
set 3	$30	8 pounds
set 4	$34	12 pounds

Using a treadmill is one way firefighters keep fit.

2 You jump rope and count your jumps. You do 35 jumps, and then you do 34 more. How many jumps in total?

When you are exercising, your heart pumps your blood around your body quicker than when you are resting. You can check your pulse to find out how fast your heart is pumping.

3 Before you start jumping rope, your heart rate is 75 beats per minute. Afterward, it goes up to 92 beats per minute. By how many beats per minute has it gone up?

4 You end your exercises by stretching on an exercise mat. Using the picture of the mat below, decide if the following statements are true or false.

48 inches long

24 inches wide

A The mat is more than 1 foot wide.

B The mat is 3 feet long.

C The width is ½ the length.

Firefighters need to be healthy and strong. A firefighter's uniform and equipment weigh about 80 pounds. That is how much the firefighter needs to lift even before rescuing anybody!

IN THE NEWS

Big fires are reported in the local newspaper. Your firefighting team is often mentioned. You talk to the reporters about what started the fire, how many people were rescued, and how you put out the fire.

YOUR LOCAL NEWS

$2 — Every Wednesday and Saturday

People Rescued from Fire!

A brave firefighter rescued five people trapped in a burning building yesterday. The building on York Road caught fire at seven o'clock last night. Nine firefighters tackled the blaze. They took one hour and eighteen minutes to put out the fire.

The people trapped in the building were led to safety by firefighter Angie Jones. Angie, age twenty-six, has been a firefighter for three years. Angie loves her job and has put out forty-eight fires so far.

The fire started at 20 York Road. It also damaged two other buildings.

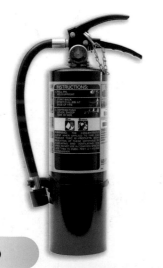

1 How much does the newspaper cost?

2 How many times per week does the paper come out?

3 How old was Angie when she first became a firefighter?

4 What is the address number of the building where the fire started?

Look at the newspaper report. All of the numbers have been written as words. Answer these questions, giving your answers in figures.

5 How many firefighters fought the fire?

6 How old is Angie Jones?

7 How long did it take the firefighters to put out the fire?

8 How many fires has Angie put out?

Firefighting is dangerous. Angie carries an alarm that will beep loudly if she becomes unconscious.

STAYING SAFE

Firefighters know what to do when they see a fire. Do you? If you see a fire, you should not try to put it out. Instead, you should shout "Fire! Fire!" very loudly and get out of the building as quickly as you can. Then, tell an adult or dial 911.

HOW DID IT START?

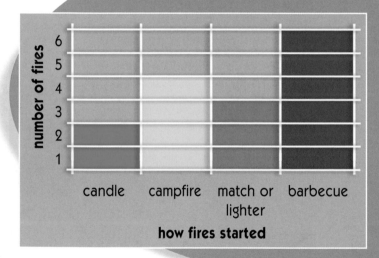

The bar graph to the left shows how some fires started.

1 How many fires were started by a match or a lighter?

2 What is the total number of fires started by campfires and barbecues?

3 What caused the least number of fires?

A

B

C

D

4 To stay safe, we must read signs and understand what they mean. What shapes are the signs above?

A danger!
B read safety instructions below this sign
C fire extinguisher
D follow the arrow to find the fire exit

The spaces between the marks on the candles to the right are each equal to 1 hour of burning time.

5 If you light candle B after candle A burns out, how long does it take both candles to burn all the way down?

6 How long would both candles be burning if you lit them both at the same time?

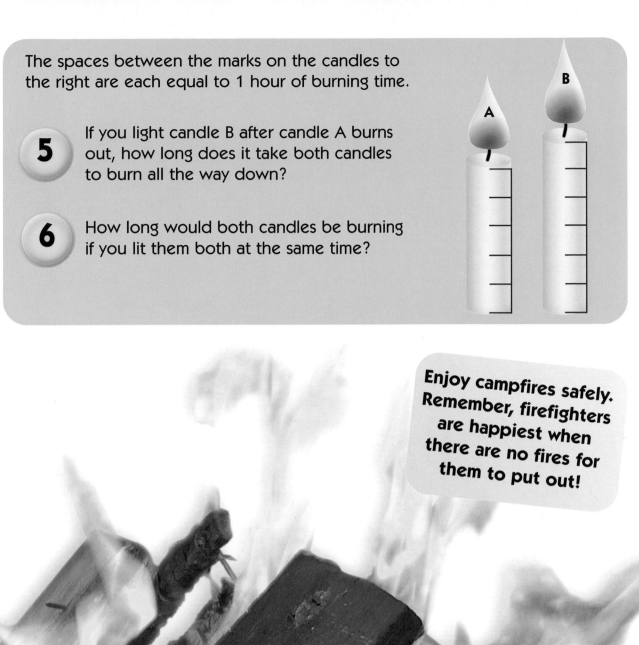

Enjoy campfires safely. Remember, firefighters are happiest when there are no fires for them to put out!

TIPS AND HELP

PAGES 6-7

Grouping and dividing - When we break up a number into equal parts or groups, each part or group is a share, or fraction, of the whole. Breaking up numbers into groups is called dividing or sharing. Here the groups are the firefighter teams.

Bar graph - A bar graph is a kind of chart used for comparing two types of information. In this bar graph, one square means one fire, and the graph compares the numbers of fires at different types of places.

PAGES 8-9

Telling time - The shorter hand on a clock is the hour hand. It shows us what hour (or "o'clock") it is. Here the hour hand is halfway between hours, so we say the time is "half past" the first of the two hours.

Difference - Finding the difference is the same as subtracting. The difference between the numbers of helmets and jackets can be written as 18 – 14. Remember that, in subtraction, we put the larger number first.

PAGES 10-11

Groups of two - When working with groups of two, it helps to learn the pattern of counting by twos, like this: 0, 2, 4, 6, 8, 10, 12, 14, 16, 18, 20, 22, 24, and so on.

Following a map - You can turn the map to follow the direction you are going. Turn the book if you need to so the road faces the direction you want to go.

PAGES 12-13

Half - The symbol for one-half is ½, which shows a 1, a line that means "shared by," and then a 2. 1 shared by 2 is ½.

PAGES 14-15

Compass points - N, E, S, W (north, east, south, west) are the points of the compass. A compass can help us find our way. We can also use a compass to talk about directions.

Pictogram - This type of chart uses a picture to show information. In this pictogram, a flame picture means 2 fires.

PAGES 16-17

Number line - The ladder is like a number line. Imagine a number on each rung. You can use the number line to count forward and backward — or up and down the ladder.

PAGES 18-19

Naming shapes - To name flat shapes, look at their sides and corners.

square: Its four sides are all the same length, and it has four right-angle corners.

rectangle: Two pairs of sides are each the same length, and it has four right-angle corners.

triangle: has only three sides

circle: Every point on a circle is the same distance from the center of the circle.

Scales - In math, scales help us see measurements. Check the scale to see what type of measurement is shown. This scale, for example, measures pounds.

PAGES 20-21

Measuring with a ruler - Be careful to place the ruler so the 0 (zero) is exactly at one end of the line to be measured. Then you can read the number on the ruler at the other end of the line.

PAGES 22-23

Clockwise - is the direction the hands of a clock move.

Counterclockwise - is the opposite direction.

PAGES 24-25

Reading a table - A table collects information in lists. The lists are side by side, and we can compare them. In this table, you can compare the four sets of hand weights.

Foot - There are 12 inches in 1 foot.

PAGES 26-27

Words for numbers - Numbers can be written in words, such as "one," "two," "three," and in figures or symbols. We use only ten symbols to write all numbers. The symbols are 0, 1, 2, 3, 4, 5, 6, 7, 8, and 9. The placement of each symbol shows its value. The 1 in the number 123 is 1 hundred, in 12 it is 1 ten, and in 31 it is 1 unit, or one.

PAGES 28-29

Signs - It is important to be able to read signs. Look for them in buildings, on the street, and in your home. Signs are often warnings or directions. Look also at the shapes of the signs because, often, certain types of signs are always the same shape.

ANSWERS

PAGES 6-7

1. 8 people
2. 30 more big fires
3. 75 fires
4. 4 fires
5. 15 fires

PAGES 8-9

1. 3 days
2. 8:30 a.m.
3. checking the engine
4. training
5. eating lunch
6. 2 hours
7. 4 more jackets
8. 18 more trousers

PAGES 10-11

1. A and E
2. 10 groups of 2
3. 6 minutes
4. C

PAGES 12-13

1. 6 vehicles
2. 2 miles
3. 90 times
4. fire engine
5. tree
6. square 12
7. campfire

PAGES 14-15

1. no
2. yes
3. as campfires
4. 20 fires
5. 11 trees are dead

PAGES 16-17

1. 10 feet higher
2. rung 2
3. rung 8
4. 15 gallons
5. 9 hoses

PAGES 18-19

1. A = triangle
   B = rectangle
   C = rectangles
   D = square
   E = circle
2. 8 minutes
3. 60 pounds
4. 180 pounds
5. right hand

PAGES 20-21

1. 1 red hose and 1 black hose
2. 3 black hoses
3. 2 inches wide
4. C
5. 6

PAGES 22-23

1. 6 rooms
2. counterclockwise
3. B $\frac{1}{3}$
4. A = 13
   B = 4
   C = 20
   D = 2

PAGES 24-25

1. set 3
2. 69 jumps
3. 17 beats per minute
4. A = true
   B = false
   C = true

PAGES 26-27

1. $2 (two dollars)
2. 2 times per week
3. 23 years old
4. 20
5. 9 firefighters
6. 26 years old
7. 1 hour and 18 minutes
8. 48 fires

PAGES 28-29

1. 3 fires
2. 10 fires
3. candles
4. A = triangle
   B = circle
   C = square
   D = rectangle
5. 11 hours
6. 5 hours